AUTHENTIC**ALLY**

Ditch the Guilt, Stop Performing, and Take Purposeful
Action as an Ally for Racial Equity

Brandi M. Baldwin, PhD

Leader-ish Publishing

Published by Leader-ish Publishing, an imprint of Leader-ish Media, LLC located at PO Box 1051, Drexel Hill, PA 19026 and online at www.leaderishmedia.com. Any internet addresses, phone numbers, or company or product information printed in this book are offered as a resource and are not intended in any way to be or to imply an endorsement by Leader-ish Publishing, nor does Leader-ish Publishing vouch for the existence, content, or services of these sites, phone numbers, companies, or products beyond the life of this book.

Cover image by: Nathan Dumlao
ISBN 979-8-7229-1953-3
Printed in the United States of America
1 2 3 4 5 6 7 8 9 10

To Well-Meaning Allies,

*The journey toward equity requires an unrelenting commitment to **unity**. A disciplined commitment that will motivate you to be kind, even when others around you are filled with hatred. A commitment that will inspire you to find healing, when others are trapped in their misery. One that inspires you to keep learning, even when others around you have stopped seeking wisdom.*

*Above all else, this journey will also require a commitment to **authenticity**. A commitment to surrender what you are for what you could become. As you read, look not for answers, but for revelation, new meaning-- a key that could very well unlock a door to deeper understanding about who you are and how you can be an ally.*

-Dr. Brandi

FORWARD

EMILIO OSORIA, FOUNDER & CEO

CURIOSITYLED.COM

Equity and social justice have taken center stage in our society, but instead of clarity, we are bombarded with conflicting views and practices, diversity equity and Inclusion "experts" coming out of the woodwork, exclusion in the name of inclusion, and ineffective training programs that don't move the needle for your business, your allyship, or society as a whole. Many want to help, but they don't know what to do, who to listen to, or where to start.

In Authentic Ally, Dr. Brandi Baldwin does not propose a new theoretical framework or competency model. She has a much higher purpose in this writing. Dr. Brandi wants to make the world a better place for all of us. Her message is simple; everyone deserves the right to equitable access to resources, information, and decision-making opportunities.

It is no accident that Dr. Brandi uses curiosity to highlight the importance of being an authentic ally. Being curiosity-led builds strong cultures, creates shared values, creates trust among team members, and most importantly, it helps us maintain a hunger for deeper understanding. Being courageous enough to **not** have all of the answers, and being curious enough to ask great questions is the cornerstone of genuine allyship.

As the CEO of Curiosity Led, we help our clients learn the art of asking better questions. As Dr. Brandi demonstrates in this book, we use **inquiry** to guide our problem-solving efforts. We guide clients through a transformative process that teaches them how curiosity-led decision making can lead to powerful business outcomes. We have to become more curious to remain competitive, innovative, and adaptable to the world that is changing so rapidly around us.

In her previous book Put In Work: Gain Respect, Influence Others, and Get Results as a New Leader, Dr. Brandi explains the importance of self-awareness and self-governance to achieve success, as demonstrated in this quote, "Masterful communication requires you to become aware of...the things you believe are acceptable and unacceptable..." This is where your allyship journey begins.

Authentic Allies must be genuinely curious about themselves and other people, be willing to change, and support others in doing the same.

Winston Churchill would have understood Dr. Brandi's message because he clearly understood the value and necessity of allyship when he stated, "There is at least one thing worse than fighting with allies – And that is to fight without them." As you embark on your journey into Authentic Allyship, keep these prerequisites in mind: 1) Be genuinely curious about yourself, others, and your community, 2) Be open to the possibility that you may have it all wrong, 3) Be willing to make mistakes, and 4) Be willing to share your journey with others.

Table of Contents

INTRODUCTION

Authentic: in accordance with an emotionally appropriate, significant,

purposive, and responsible mode of human life.

In our fake phony and filtered world, there's no wonder why authenticity as a core value is almost nonexistent these days. We no longer honor our *authentic* selves. We don't push past our own discomfort to speak the truth. We don't seek opportunities to connect with people who will accept us as we are. We'd rather adjust who we *really* are so that we can be accepted by other (equally inauthentic) people.

We perform for our coworkers, our friends, and even our closest family members. We resist rejection from others by rejecting ourselves first. We'll trade our dignity to say and do things that are unethical, if it'll lead to our acceptance. We'll go with the majority of wrongdoers instead of standing alone in righteousness. We'll stay silent and follow, instead of speaking up to lead. We are biased toward our own self-interests, while claiming that we care about the self-interests of others. We are blatant hypocrites with no commitment to a consistent set of virtuous ideologies. And yet we think we're ready to be authentic allies for racial equity?

The Inspiration Behind Authentic Ally

In the Summer of 2020, a video of a police officer using excessive force to restrain a Black man during an arrest went viral. This police officer's actions ultimately led to the death of the civilian and the public outrage spread like wildfire. While people from all backgrounds were disgusted and appalled at what happened, the backlash for this particular incident spread to social media, and I immediately saw offense, hatred, and rage spewing toward White people. The intensity of the dialogue (if you can even call it dialogue) was at a never-before-seen level. The social scientist in me wanted to dig deeper into what I was seeing as this was surely a new social dynamic that hit our professional spaces.

What resulted over the next few weeks was a huge divide. A divide in perspectives, a divide in experiences, and a divide in the spaces that we had to share--our workplaces, our homes, and even within our families. However, in the midst of this divide I also saw a groundswell of unity. White professionals sprang into action to support their Black/African American comrades. Alas, the racial equity movement was invigorated in a new way! Or was it?

The stage had now been set for true change, but unfortunately, it seemed that everyone was simply auditioning to give their best allyship performance. Supposed "allies" were on self-centered social media campaigns to draw attention, not to the cause, but to themselves. You know them. They were posting black squares online, using all of the trending hashtags, and targeting any and everyone who hadn't done the same. The level of self-deprecation was also at an all-time high. Companies even got in on the marketing blitz to let the world know how much they cared about racial equity. Hundreds of millions of dollars were being donated to any organization that claimed to help Black people. Allyship had gone mainstream, but I was still left wondering what the long-term positive impact would be.

Today, the many allies who stepped up so eagerly have since lost steam. Allyship fatigue has set in and their efforts have been reduced to attending webinar after webinar on the same topics. They are aimlessly searching for answers to questions they often can't even articulate. I've concluded that many inauthentic allies are actually trying to find answers that will help them *feel* better, not answers that will actually help them support the racial equity movement. They are burnt out because they're still trying to figure out how to "do" allyship, when the truth is that they need to focus on simply *being* allies. When you just **are** an ally, you don't have to think about it. You don't have to turn your allyship switch on and off.

So, what is happening in the world of allyship these days? In my estimate, there are droves of allies still claiming to be working on addressing their "unconscious biases". Unfortunately, this group will be on the "unconscious bias" hamster wheel for years before they realize that being aware of their biases won't actually help them remove them.

Another group of allies is most-likely still engaged in their personal "anti-racism" work, which is interesting when most of these allies had never heard of that term before the Summer of 2020. Working on becoming an "anti-racist" is the hottest trend right now, however, very few people know that the concept has been around for decades and has never reached this level of mainstream attention due to its many limitations. I could write an entire book on this by the way, but let's stick to the task at hand.

The last remnant of allies are, well, over it. They've lost steam and they *would* be active and authentic allies if they just had the tools. Their interest is waning and they've re-prioritized being an ally for racial equity a bit further down on their social action to-do list. Wherever you are as an ally, my goal is to engage in a discussion to help you build a solid foundation that will sustain your allyship journey for years to come.

The Authentic Ally Lens

In Authentic Ally, I argue that most well-meaning allies are not as ready as they think they are to step up to support the racial equity movement. Before allies launch out to help "eradicate racial inequities", they must plan, prepare, and address the knowledge gaps and personal insecurities that may derail their allyship journey.

It's important to note that this book is not written from a social justice lens. It is written from a psycho-social lens and is informed by interpersonal and relational communication theories, which focus on observing and changing human social behavior. Don't worry, this book is less about theory and more about practice. I spared you the "theoretical underpinnings" of what informs my lens and purposely jumped straight to sharing ideas and actions that can help you change today. My audience for this book are not my scholarly peers, they are not other practitioners in this space. This book is for the average professional interested in allyship.

What I know for sure is that when you provide people with information, they can use to mature their perspective and change their mind, you can positively impact their behavior within the varied social contexts that they occupy. When people change their behaviors for long enough, they are able to seamlessly incorporate those new behaviors into consistent habits that take far less effort. The racial equity movement will need allies for years to come, and I know that sustaining purposeful allyship action requires less doing and more being.

This book is for the well-meaning allies who are ready to acknowledge that even 1% of their approach has been pretentious, inauthentic, performed, or with inauthentic motives. As an ally, have you ever acted out of guilt, shame, embarrassment, sadness, anger, or fear? If so, this book is definitely for you. Aspiring authentic allies who allow themselves to be vulnerable will have the best results after reading this book.

A Guilt-Free Guide

It's disturbing to see how many people, in their desperation for answers, are reading and accepting the countless texts, articles, and books that are riddled with hateful ideologies.

These texts seem to have a lot of strong ideas with minimal practical suggestions. These authors can identify every flaw and point the blame at others, but rarely provide sustainable actions that we can take to move to a solution-oriented approach.

Authentic Ally is a guilt-free guide and a no judgement zone. My goal is to call you up, not call you out. Yes, we will address some challenging topics, but there's nothing in this text that should make a well-meaning ally feel "less than". Nothing here should make you feel shameful or guilty. This book is about moving forward, letting go of the past, and searching for opportunities to think differently so that you can seize positive opportunities for your future.

I employ candor, honesty, and accountability to put a mirror up to the inauthentic mindsets of well-meaning allies that undermine their success as allies for racial equity.

Guiding Principles of The Book

It's important that you are aware of what the guiding principles are of this book. Let's review a few of those principles now.

Everyone Can Be an Ally

It's time to dispel the myth that White professionals are the only target group who need to learn about allyship and racial equity. In its purest form, an ally is someone who you enter into an alliance with. We all can and should be allies for racial equity.

Equity for All & Equity First

Too many well-meaning allies are so focused on the D in DEI (diversity, equity, and inclusion). They hastily rush to "brownify" their boards, promote the next "person of color", and highlight diversity in their marketing campaigns. What most leaders neglect is the **equity** part of the equation. Sure, your organization *looks* more diverse, but are there systems and processes in place to ensure that everyone's pay is equitable, that their opportunities for advancement are equitable? Never spend more time on diversity than you do on equity. There are many places with lots of representation and very little equity.

Micro-level Change Leads to Macro-level Change

I often hear overly ambitious (and naive) allies who adamantly claim that they want to "tear down America's racist systems of oppression", yet, months later they can't even articulate how they've positively impacted one "system of oppression".

The truth is that we don't have to "tear down" systems if we transform them from the inside out. We don't have to #cancel, fight, and post about inequities, when we can use our own social influence within our communities to *be* more equitable ourselves. Today's allies must shift their focus away from others and inward toward themselves to make quantum progress for the racial equity movement.

Cultural Competence is the Goal

With so many people confused (but still committed) to this whole "anti-racism" approach, I'd like to offer an alternative lens that is proven to have positive outcomes for people around the world. Rather than anyone trying to be anti-racist, I recommend that allies focus on building their cultural competence.

Cultural Competence is a continuous and lifelong journey to increase your skills in being proficient in intercultural and intra cultural knowledge which can improve the ability to work with people who are different from you.

All professionals should be working actively to increase their cultural competence. We all have something to learn about each other. When you focus on building your cultural competence you will automatically minimize occurrences of unintentional microaggressions, racial insults, culturally insensitive statements, and general interpersonal flubs. If you build your cultural competence, you will be less likely to make an offensive comment to someone of a different background. When you build your cultural competence, you will be able to empathize with others' personal experiences.

Choose to Have a Positive Psychological Orientation

An ally's psychological orientation to this work is very important, and I've found in my study of psycho-social processes that when people are trying to "fight against" anything, they tend to lose sight of what exactly they're fighting for. This win-lose orientation often cripples the ally's efforts, making their "fight" an uphill battle filled with perceived barriers and stumbling blocks all put in their way by " evil others" who just "don't get it". I argue that every ally should exchange their "fight against" orientation with an "advocate for" orientation. When you are "for" something it becomes an initiative that you can look forward to. It becomes something that energizes you--something that you look forward to. I urge all allies to shift your thinking so that your allyship journey has the longevity required to have an impact for decades to come.

Conclusion

So, the question still remains, are you ready? Only you know if you're ready to begin the journey toward authentic allyship. If the answer is yes, continue reading. If you're unsure, continue reading. On the other hand, if you've hated most of what I've shared so far, if you've already identified multiple things that I'm "wrong" about; stop reading now. Put the book down and come back when you are operating from a learning posture. Come back when you're open to changing **your** actions and behaviors. I'm not going anywhere, and I'll be here ready to continue the conversation when you are.

*KEY TERMINOLOGY

This book will not include foundational information or definitions of basic DEI-related terminology. If you are not familiar with these terms, I'd recommend that you take a few minutes to look up the definitions of the following words:

- Diversity
- Equity
- Inclusion
- Equality
- Cultural Competence
- Ally (original definition)

BRANDI M. BALDWIN

**Ditch the Guilt, Stop Performing, and Take
Purposeful Action as an Ally for Racial Equity**

Part One

Authentic vs. Counterfeit Allyship

BRANDI M. BALDWIN

CHAPTER 1

CALLING ALL ALLIES

As the Founder and Sr. Partner of the Calling All Allies Project, a DEI innovation and organizational equity firm, I've worked with thousands of professionals from around the world. I'm constantly listening to how people are thinking about this topic. I get to hear from real professionals who are trying to wrap their heads around their newly found awareness of racial equity issues. Our work is guided by the idea that what happens is not as important as *how we respond* to what happens. And so today, I ask you. How have you been responding? How have you been showing up? Have you been modeling the behavior that you want to see from others in the world? If so, great! If not, make a commitment to do better.

At the Calling All Allies Project our goal is to help companies and professionals push the limits of their thinking around diversity, equity, and inclusion. Our tagline is "Ignite Workplace Unity" which is our number one goal. After the events of 2020 however, the DEI field changed dramatically. DEI "experts" are no longer adhering to the foundational principles of organizational development, change management, and employee engagement to help their clients. They are not bringing their professional selves to work; they are now bringing their personal selves to their work. The majority of today's DEI practitioners can barely separate their personal beliefs from the work that they do. This is eroding the industry and diminishing the standard of excellence that was once present. My hope is that we can quickly recalibrate and stabilize the industry standards that will guide our work for years to come.

Opened Mouths and Closed Minds

The loudest media narratives have become "truths", and there has been a reckless abandonment of the things that brought the DEI industry this far. We now see DEI "experts" blatantly endorsing exclusionary strategies as a part of supposed inclusion initiatives. Employees are walking on eggshells, scared to say anything for fear that it may get them socially ostracized or fired. People are no longer authentically engaging in the uncomfortable dialogue required to forge true progress. Thoughtful disagreements are a thing of the past.

Today, we're stuck with open mouths and closed minds. Inauthentic allies don't really want to learn. They just want to hear people validate their own feelings. They want to be "right", and of course someone else has to be wrong. I've learned first-hand how challenging it is to open people's minds to new ways of thinking about racial equity.

In the Spring of 2021, I remember encountering my first media crisis in over 10 years of being in business. My name hit international headlines after I facilitated a workshop as a subcontractor for another DEI firm in the city. They'd been working with a local organization who was digging themselves out of years of organizational dysfunction. I was brought in to help all of their employees build cultural competence skills with three presentations that happened over two days.

During the first presentation, I started discussing the power of language, and that's when the conversation began to deteriorate. A handful of employees were so furious at the viewpoint I was presenting that they went to the media. Yes, the media! Not the workshop evaluation, not to the internal leadership, not to the organizers of the event, they called an insider at the media to "tattle" on Dr. Brandi. A few employees from the first session were so emotionally unhinged, talking them out of their revenge mission would have been a futile effort. An article was published and went viral less than 5 days later.

After reading the article that was published and reposted on other national and international platforms, I responded with a public statement that reflects the current challenges of this work. Here's an excerpt from a statement that I released about what happened:

"There was a specific segment of my workshop where we began discussing the power of language. I always challenge audiences to think about their language choices, the varied meaning of terminology, and how those language choices impact their ability to find common ground with others in the workplace. While terminology like white supremacy, white privilege and others have their own place, the effectiveness of these concepts dissolve in the workplace context when supporting organizations in doing DEI change management work. I urged the audience to think differently about their usage of these terms, especially when attempting to describe interpersonal phenomena in the workplace. Can we negate the existence of the entirety of those concepts? Of course not, but we do need to think more strategically about when and how to use certain concepts as we work to create truly inclusive company cultures. I was also attempting to challenge the group to limit the common habit of centering "whiteness" within every discussion about racial inequities, but we barely got that far.

Clarifying My Role as a DEI Consultant
The average professional cannot begin to imagine how challenging it is to do this work in a responsible way. My work is bound by the principles of DEI and I have to honor diversity,

18

equity, and inclusion at all costs. While some DEI consultants approach their work from a personal lens, using their own lived experience as a qualifier for the credibility of their work, I do not take that approach. I use evidence-based practices that have been validated by decades of research.

As an African American woman, I have been to court to fight unfair treatment that I have received by the police (won the case by the way), I have been discriminated against while pursuing my doctoral degree, I have been excluded from purchasing property in certain neighborhoods by real estate agents, and I encounter discrimination (call it racism if you want to) regularly, especially in this field. Despite every right that I may have to use these experiences as a back-drop for my DEI expertise, I've been able to get far more RESULTS for organizations by utilizing an organizational development and change management approach that is grounded within a psycho-social framework.

In the news article that was published and repurposed many times, I was characterized as demonstrating "anti-Blackness" for discussing the fact that "white privilege" does not exist as an absolute. All of our "privilege" is contextual. This fact is not used to "placate" anyone (as the article asserts), rather, it is used to help professionals better understand how fluid and flexible these social constructs are. Because remember, they are social constructs, right? Once we acknowledge this, we have the power to redefine our experiences. So no, I'm not "divorced from reality", and definitely not suffering from "anti-Blackness" or "internalized racism" for taking this approach. I know that it's hard for people NOT to see me as a "Black DEI Consultant". I am definitely prejudged and expected to show up in a certain way because of my race, but that's par for the course in this work.

Where Do We Go From Here?
With the rise of "us vs. them" DEI consulting practices, my team purposely chooses to reject that approach. I don't believe that white allies have to participate in sitting through a "reckoning" as a sort of rights-of-passage for them to learn how to support the racial equity movement. Companies will never be able to create a truly "safe place" for these types of discussions if they employ a method that requires one group to be characterized as "bad" just by the virtue of their skin color. Does individual character mean anything anymore?

We have a saying, "people love to learn, but hate to change", and there's a method to pushing the limits and taking a purposefully unexpected approach. While I fully see that this approach isn't the best fit for certain organizations, I'm proud to have worked nationally and internationally with organizations of all sizes who are willing to push through their personal discomfort to move toward equity. While I'm disheartened that the emotions of a few led to this, I'm hopeful that this situation will create an opportunity to continue the discussion around how we can all work together to advance diversity, equity, and inclusion."

A group of angry allies, upset that I didn't show up with a stereotypical "Black DEI consultant" narrative, colluded with the media on a smear campaign that went viral and could've permanently damaged my business. All of this because they were trying to be "allies for racial equity"? This is the absurdity of what the current allyship landscape looks like. I am a professional on the front lines of innovating in the DEI space, so I can take this kind of heat, but what about the average person who tries to engage with others, but is met with so much hatred and resistance that they just give up? What about the well-meaning allies who are learning how to build their cultural competence? They don't have the mental fortitude to put up with these types of low EQ (emotional competence) individuals. This is why I've written this book.

The ugly truth is that people say that they want to change, but they don't. People say that they want inclusion, but they don't.

People say that they want equity, but they don't. They would rather spend their energy calling the media on someone who doesn't think like them, then channeling that energy into changing their own behavior.

Final Thoughts

The DEI industry is maturing. Gone are the days when you can throw unconscious bias training and a "cultural sensitivity" workshop at people and think it'll spark long-term positive change. I implore today's DEI consultants, HR leaders, and OD practitioners to remain steadfast and unmovable as you navigate the wild west that has become the DEI industry. Double down on the principles that have worked and resist the pressure to succumb to the latest trends that cause divisiveness within companies. Leave your political p.o.v. at the door and get back to helping organizations increase their employee engagement, inclusion, and performance by using an integrated DEI approach.

As professionals, we have to think strategically. We have to be innovative. We have to choose a new narrative. We have to change *our* behaviors to change our organizations. We have to realize that changing ourselves is the first step in this process.

So, I'm calling you. I'm calling all of the allies out there who are ready to ignite workplace unity, ignite family unity, and ignite community unity. Together we can have a big impact.

CHAPTER 2

CHARACTERISTICS OF

INAUTHENTIC ALLIES

B y now, you've definitely encountered an inauthentic ally. Heck, you may be a recovering inauthentic ally yourself. There's no judgment here, but we do need to discuss a few things so that you know how to correct or avoid some of these pitfalls.

Inauthentic allies suffer from a cognitive distortion that often leads to their inability to consider and actively address their own shortcomings. The inauthentic ally views themselves as right (and even righteous at times) in their pursuit to help others.

Unfortunately, because they've chosen to operate from this lens, they tend to become unraveled when they encounter others with differing perspectives. Conversations quickly deteriorate as these allies become more and more determined to be right.

Inauthentic Ally Types

So, what types of characteristics are common among inauthentic allies? I've put together a short list of (unofficial) "inauthentic allyship types" that will be referenced in this chapter and in other parts of the book. Keep in mind that these types are not mutually exclusive. You may observe an ally with characteristics of more than one type, or you may notice a bit more subtlety in their actions than I've described here.

Remember, the purpose of the next section is to identify and outline inauthentic allyship behaviors that you need to identify within yourself. While you may recognize a few of these characteristics in your colleagues, please don't use the list as a way to call people out. Oh, and I'm giving you fair warning not to take my inauthentic ally titles too seriously. You'll see some humor in the titles, but just roll with it. Focus on the behaviors and actions I'm describing.

The Moral Superiority Superstar

This ally thinks they are morally superior to all other allies. If there were an ally ranking system, they would put themselves at the top. These allies look for opportunities to flex their moral superiority in conversations, at events, and on social media. They are constantly patting themselves on the back and demonizing others for not "getting it". In conversations you'll hear them talking about how sad it is that others "just don't understand how serious racial equity work is". If you do not give the Moral Superiority Superstar the credit they think they deserve, they will quickly snub their nose at you, label you as a part of the problem, and dismiss anything you have to say as irrelevant or out of touch. Their primary goal is to not be seen as a part of the "bad" group. In this "fight" (because everything is a fight to this type of ally), they've created a mental construct that only allows for good and bad players to be a part of this game called life. You're either one or the other, and they will not, under any circumstances be a part of the "bad" group.

Unfortunately, this psychological positioning limits their ability to see that anything they're doing (or thinking) is flawed. These are the toughest inauthentic allies to help. Their lack of humility blocks their ability to evolve their allyship into something more genuine.

The On-Trend Friend

The On-Trend Friend is the ally whose main objective is to keep up with the latest racial equity trends. They are a friendlier version of the Woke-ology Professor (which we'll talk about in a second).

This inauthentic ally gets most of their racial equity information from social media. They've pinned and bookmarked every info-graphic, news article, and post from a buffet of sources that they use to stay on-trend at all times. They will be the first one using new woke-cabulary terms. They present as all over the place from month to month as they shift, adjust, and transition from one new concept to the next. Black square on social media. They did it. Trending hashtags, they use them. In conversation, their inauthenticity is more subtle than The Moral Superiority Superstar. However, there's still a twinge of "I know something you don't know" that shows up when you engage with them. Their primary goal is to not be perceived as being uninformed about racial equity topics. Their strategy is to learn a little bit about a lot of things so that at any moment they have a fact, book recommendation, or vocabulary correction to offer you. The On-Trend Friend does a lot of talking and not nearly enough listening. Their talking is used to mask their own insecurity about being an ally for racial equity.

The Anti-Racism Radical

The Anti-Racism Radical is easy to spot. This inauthentic ally has gone from not being aware of even the most basic racial inequities in society to becoming a full blown anti-racist expert in a few months. These allies found and studied this one concept and now believe that every racial inequity can be solved with "anti-racism work". Better opportunities needed for people of color in STEM? Anti-racism work. More funding for high-need schools? Anti-racism work. Creating a more inclusive environment at my company. Anti-racism work.

If you're not doing anti-racism work, it's a huge problem for these types. The irony with the Anti-Racism Radical is that this is the one inauthentic ally type that is typically the most confused about how to translate anti-racism work into actual results. They often spend months doing "anti-racism" work for themselves and within their companies, only to emerge months later with nothing more to offer than a set of random things that they've participated in, which offer no clear measurable outcomes. But because they've invested so much in hinging their allyship bets on anti-racism work, they feel obligated to continue on the same path, rather than accepting that perhaps they need to find another way. To-date, I have yet to hear from or see a credible and successful example of an ally who can articulate that their "anti-racism" work really helped them accomplish a significant positive change for themselves or others.

Rather, this ally is merely a near cousin to the On-Trend Friend. Someone who won't allow themselves to accept the truth that no **one** solution will fix all racial equity issues. This ally made the "inauthentic ally" list because despite their best efforts in claiming that they want to see racial equity, their allegiance is to the **concept** of anti-racism first. It's a badge of honor. "I'm an anti-racist". And because they've made it a part of their identity, they rarely are willing to give it up to search for other methodologies that can actually support racial equity for the communities they claim to care about.

The Guilty Guy/Gal

The Guilty Guy/Gal is stuck in a seemingly permanent state of guilt, shame, and sadness for all of those "poor marginalized people". These allies have fully immersed themselves in learning about other cultures, however, their approach has focused on most of the bad that has happened. They haven't balanced their perspective and thus, they are convinced that the other group is so "damaged", so "broken", so "victimized" that their allyship behaviors are all coming from a place of extreme guilt and sadness.

The Guilty Guy/Gal quickly becomes infatuated with helping and advocating for the "marginalized" people, so much so that they develop a savior complex as an attempt to soothe that nagging sense of guilt that has developed within them. Ironically, they are also simultaneously creating an unintentional superiority complex. Their superiority complex develops as a defense mechanism that helps them cope with these feelings of guilt and shame. Unfortunately, this newly developed mindset tends to reinforce the notion that the other group (whichever group that is) is perpetually inferior, while reinforcing the notion that they themselves are superior. This cognitive distortion locks these inauthentic ally types into an unproductive cycle of emotion-based actions that are less focused on the racial equity movement and more focused on feeding their own insecurities.

The Thought Police

With so much chatter about defunding the police, I'd like to start a petition to defund the Thought Police. These inauthentic ally types have one goal and one goal only--to get everyone to think like them. They pretend to care about diversity, but the idea of *diversity of thought* doesn't fit within this equation. They are the allies that will exclude you in the name of inclusion. Why? Because to them, anyone who has a different perspective than theirs is dangerous, not credible, not worthy of being a part of the discussion. Their primary playground is social media, although you'll find these types at work too. The Thought Police have precincts set up on Facebook, IG, and even LinkedIn. They troll posts and make sure to keep a close eye on keeping others in-check by demonizing them for having their own perspective.

The goal of the Thought Police ally is to be understood, not to understand. They can't have two conflicting thoughts in their heads at the same time. It's never both/and. They really don't like it when their ideas are challenged. Similar to their cousin, the Moral Superiority Superstar, these ally types are performing as a self-appointed allyship authority figure to cover up their own insecurities. Combine this style with a person who has a low EQ and you'll have a Captain of the Thought Police on your hands. Their unwillingness to seek common ground limits this ally from seeing and fixing their own blind spots. One of which being their own oppressive nature.

The Political Polarizer

The Political Polarizer uses their allyship as a cover to promote their political ideologies. It's evident with a brief conversation that these inauthentic allies already have a clear political perspective and narrative that they hold near and dear to their heart. That's fine. No judgment there. What's problematic, is that the Political Polarizer is putting their political agenda ahead of a true agenda for racial equity. You will notice in conversation that they will mention political issues, trash politicians that they hate, and use only the most popular political current event as a backdrop for their allyship discussions.

The biggest blind spot with the Political Polarizer is that they lack the self-awareness and common sense to realize that people of all backgrounds have diverse political ideologies. Their overconfidence in assuming that "we all" agree with their political perspectives is damaging to their allyship work. These inauthentic allies don't even realize how many people they've shared their righteous political ideologies with, who actually don't agree.

The Woke-ology Professor

Welcome to Woke University, established in 2020 by a group of woke-ivists who have now expanded to campuses located in Wokeville, Woke Town, Woke-adelphia, Woke-lanta, and Woke-kanda. Your Woke-ology Professor will equip you with all of the classic courses that you will need to get your Master's (oops, I forgot they don't use that term anymore due to the slavery connotation), ahem, your graduate certificate in Woke-ology.

Courses like, "If You're White, You're Not Right", "Psychopathology of the Karen", and "Dismantling Systemically Oppressive, Privileged, Superior, Supreme, Codified, Blatant, Nuanced, Ideological Frameworks of a non Anti-Racist American Regime for BIPOC Nationalist Survivors of Inequality". Tuition is free, and upon completion of the program, you will be able to use your degree... NOWHERE (spoiler alert).

The Woke-ology Professor is the most contradictory inauthentic ally of them all. While arguing that White supremacy is an issue, they'll simultaneously argue that White people have inherent and absolute privileges based on the color of their skin (the lie detector determined, that is a lie). While arguing that "dismantling systems of oppression" is necessary, they often work for, economically patronize, and strive to be a part of those same "systems" (I can write an entire book on this point alone).

The Woke-ology Professor often makes sweeping

generalizations and accusations about broad groups of people. They are seemingly incapable of approaching their allyship in a nuanced way, partly because they, like the On-Trend Friend, have only a superficial disintegrated understanding of the concepts that make up their own value system.

It's like these allies are following a script. Their biggest tell is their language. These inauthentic allies all sound alike. The disconcerting part about the Woke-ology Professor is that they are typically fueled by anger that stems from their own unresolved issues. They have either been bullied, abused, rejected, or excluded in some way during their childhood, early adult life, or at the hands of an employer or other significant figure. They are attracted to this movement and any movement for the "underdogs", the "disenfranchised". When this inauthentic ally is raising their fists in the air, chanting and screaming for racial equity, they are actually crying out for their own voice to be heard. They are often channeling their own unresolved pain to "fight" for the cause of racial equity. Racial equity is not their goal. Finally having an outlet to release their pent-up anger, frustration, and sadness is.

What The Woke-ology Professor doesn't understand is that much of their ideology reinforces the very concepts that they call oppressive. These inauthentic allies are typically on an exhausting hamster wheel of low-impact actions that never seem to transition from talk to more purposeful strategic action. They are the call out kings and queens. You will get called out, put out, kicked out, and drowned out by this bunch. Beware.

Final Thoughts

True allyship has to be pure. Allies for racial equity have to sincerely be working toward advancing the goals of the communities they seek to serve. Let's reflect for a moment. Did you see yourself in any of these types? Have you observed any of these behaviors in others? What specific behaviors can you remove from your practice after reviewing some of the inauthentic ally types? What is your next step?

BRANDI M. BALDWIN

CHAPTER 3

PEOPLE LOVE TO LEARN, BUT HATE TO CHANGE

L earning and self-education mean nothing if you're not willing to take action to change your **own** behaviors. I see so many "allies" for racial equity focused intently on working to change the behaviors of others. They watch a few documentaries, register for as many DEI webinars as possible, read a LinkedIn article on racism, tune in to hear what their favorite millionaire celebrity or politician is saying about inequality, and BOOM, they've done it. They have put themselves through a PhD in DEI and suddenly, they are the judge and jury for everyone else's allyship journey.

The key to authentic allyship is having a laser-focused approach that starts with looking inward and correcting one's own biases, flaws, and lack of information. If all well-meaning allies for racial equity focused on themselves first, we'd see a lot more tangible progress happening in this space.

The Authentic Ally Approach

The Authentic Ally operates from a mindset that is distinctly different from the mindset of the Inauthentic Ally. In the next section, I've outlined how the Authentic Ally psychologically orients themselves toward their racial equity work. This approach creates the self-awareness and personal accountability required to sustain a long-term authentic allyship strategy that actually gets results. After a few months, the Inauthentic Ally often burns out and loses focus and traction on their racial equity goals. This approach does just the opposite.

The Authentic Ally Leans into the Discomfort

Being an ally for racial equity is tough work. It requires such a high level of self-awareness, discipline, emotional competence, and psychological resilience that the average person picks a new cause to champion within months. Rather than being discouraged or turned off by the discomfort of being an ally for racial equity, Authentic Allies lean into the discomfort of it all.

Feeling comfortable is so overrated. I hear professionals talking about their idealistic vision for a day when everyone will feel "comfortable" in their workplace. A day in the future when we can all feel "comfortable" having "tough" conversations about race, and so on. That day will happen, as soon as everyone begins to think alike. Unfortunately, there will never be a time in our future when we all think alike (thank goodness).

This idealistic, yet highly illogical perspective makes comfort the goal, rather than mutual respect. The Authentic Ally is willing and able to lean into their discomfort because their focus is not on comfort at all, it's on purposefully stretching the limits of their current understanding about what it means to be an ally. The close-minded rigid ally lashes out or shuts down when they feel discomfort. The open-minded ally makes their personal growth a priority, not their comfort.

The Authentic Ally Understands Their Role

Inauthentic Allies are often misguided about what their role is in the movement for racial equity. They think they have to change minds, educate others, fight "the Man", and protect those "poor marginalized people" who haven't been given a "fair chance to succeed".

The Authentic Ally knows that their role is to support the goals of those who they are trying to help. In order to do that effectively, they must be active listeners (not talkers) who are working together with the community they want to support.

For example, I've had countless private conversations with my African American friends who are perplexed, baffled even at the actions they've observed from Inauthentic Allies trying to support racial equity in America. From seeing racial equity protests with more White people than non-White people, to wondering who #canceled some of our favorite books, brands, thought leaders, and celebrities without our permission, to White-owned corporation donating hundreds of millions of dollars to organizations who to-date have not shown "receipts" on how those millions were used to directly support the African American community, to out-of-touch allies advocating for law enforcement reform that would further endanger families living in high-crime areas. And the list goes on. The danger of Inauthentic Allies not knowing (or accepting) their roles, is that they can easily begin to make decisions on-behalf of people and communities that did not ask for their "help".

The Authentic Ally knows that their role becomes defined AFTER they've done the work to identify which Allyship Domain (see Ch. 5) is best suited for the goals they are trying to achieve. Their work should be a collaborative effort with the communities they're trying to help.

The Authentic Ally Acknowledges Their Change Readiness

I've heard horror stories from people who have encountered angry, belligerent, close-minded, judgmental, elitist allies who present themselves as though they have arrived. They've made up their mind about what the problem is, who's to blame, and how it needs to be fixed. If you're not in agreement with them, you are the enemy--

their enemy. Beyond their clear lack of humility, these inauthentic allies suffer from arrested development in their allyship journey. They never quite make it past go.

They spend months badgering others from their moral high horse, only to realize that their efforts have actually deterred more people from becoming allies for this cause. No one wants to join a cause filled with a group of angry, disgruntled, emotionally unhinged complainers. No one. The Authentic Ally knows that the biggest gift they can give to this cause is showing maturity, poise, respect, and resilience that will attract and excite others about getting involved. The Authentic Ally is ready and willing to step into a truly supportive role for those in need.

The Authentic Ally Operates from Pure Motives

All motives matter. Right now, there are hundreds of thousands of inauthentic allies whose motives are not pure, and it shows. The amount of performing I've seen is ridiculous. Here are a few inauthentic motives that are unacceptable if you're trying to be an authentic ally.

- Not wanting to be seen as racist by others
- FOMO- fear of missing out on the latest trend
- To hide the fact that you actually are racist
- To stick it to "the Man"
- To punish people who you do not like

- To feel relevant
- To work out your own personal or political agenda

You must be clear about why you want to be an ally for racial equity. Only you can determine what that reason is, and only you can be responsible enough to NOT start your allyship journey until your motives are pure. It's better to take no action, than to take inauthentic action.

The Authentic Ally Checks Their Lens at the Door

Are you willing to be a true ally for racial equity, or are there conditions on your authentic participation? I've observed so many professionals who create unnecessary barriers to their own allyship journey. They are willing to be allies for African Americans, but only the ones who are a part of one particular political party. They're willing to advocate for immigration policies, as long as the policies are aligned with their political ideals. Are these allies inauthentic, absolutely, but what is more troubling is the fact that these types of allies are the most **biased** of them all.

The Authentic Ally checks their lens at the door. They are willing to temporarily put down their political and religious beliefs to help ALL groups who are disadvantaged as a result of social, economic, and interpersonal inequities. This is the highest form of sacrifice an authentic ally can make. If you claim to be an ally, yet you can't bring yourself to help or support others unless their worldview is identical to yours, quit now. Leave the movement now. Focus on another cause.

The Authentic Ally Uses Critical Thinking Skills

There is no recipe or formula. There's no such thing as allyship-in-a-box. There isn't a quick fix. No amount of "tips and tricks" will help you with this. Authentic allyship requires critical thinking skills. It requires a willingness to try, fail, iterate, and test your assumptions, ideas, behaviors, and interactions.

So many well-meaning allies for racial equity have exhausted themselves by attending every single workshop or webinar that they can in this endless search for the final missing piece that will help it all "click". That will help it all make sense, so that they can have a blueprint for what to do to help, to fix things, to feel better about being an ally. Unfortunately, there is no blueprint. Much of your allyship journey will emerge organically (and rightfully so). Embrace this fact as an opportunity, not a setback.

At some point you have to start thinking for yourself. Take the allyship training wheels off. Stop being so scared to be wrong. Equip yourself with the tools to identify and combat the droves of inauthentic allies that will try to derail your personal allyship journey, and get to work. There's no amount of thinking, learning or preparation that will replace true authentic allyship in action.

Final Thoughts

It'll take a little time, but once you hone in on shifting your mindset to these principles you will notice a significant decrease in your stress, and increase in your results to reduce societal inequity within your spheres of influence.

Ditch the Guilt, Stop Performing, and Take Purposeful Action as an Ally for Racial Equity

Part Two

PREREQUISITES FOR ALLYSHIP &

DOMAINS OF ALLYSHIP

CHAPTER 4

YES, THERE ARE PREREQUISITES

FOR ALLYSHIP

D EI experts have done a great disservice to professionals by calling people to action without providing them with a foundation for how to be an ally. Their haste to galvanize as many people as possible to this cause has created a myriad of both corporate and interpersonal disasters. Like giving an untrained teenager keys to a car without a license, DEI experts have given untrained well-meaning allies the green light to do something... anything, when the first step should be providing them with insights on what exactly they need to do.

No one talks about the prerequisites for allyship. Passion just isn't enough. Caring is not a significant qualifier for those who want to be allies for racial equity. Without addressing the prerequisites, many well-meaning allies spend the first several months of their allyship journey lost, frustrated, and unsure if any of their efforts are actually helping this cause.

BRANDI M. BALDWIN

The Prerequisites for Allyship Model

I developed the Prerequisites for Allyship Model to help early-stage allies think through and respond to key inquiries that will help them create a solid foundation for their allyship journey. Each of the Prerequisites for Allyship inquiries fall within one of four categories: motives, triggers, knowledge, and influence. Let's review them now.

#1 Motives- Why do you want to be an ally?

As previously discussed, your motives are all about the rationale for why you want to be an ally for racial equity. I can't emphasize enough the importance of having pure motives. Your motivation for why you want to be an ally is probably the single **most** important factor that will determine your consistency and impact as a champion for equity.

Don't fall into the trap of wanting to be an ally because it seems like the "right" thing to do. Don't start your allyship journey because it's on trend. Don't decide to become more culturally competent to show your network that you're "woke" about issues of inequity in society and the workplace. Definitely don't become an ally because you want to be the hero that saves "those poor" INSERT GROUP HERE, who are helpless without you.

You will fail at allyship if you start this journey with the wrong intentions. When responding to this question, I recommend working to identify 2-3 motivations. With a few powerful reasons, you will have the focus and clarity required to remain consistent during your allyship journey.

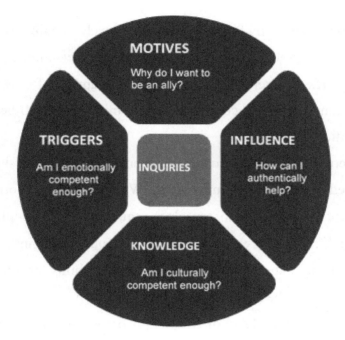

Figure 4.1

Think of your motives as your North Star. They will hold you accountable to staying focused when everyone else jumps on the next trend. They will be in the back of your mind during times when you want to quit. They will keep you from participating in low-impact allyship activities (which we will discuss in the next chapter).

Your "why?" is essential to having a successful allyship journey. When everyone else is over it, you will still be there, seeking opportunities to support this cause.

#2 Triggers- Are you emotionally competent enough?

Being an authentic ally for racial equity can be challenging. Between educating yourself, having uncomfortable conversations, seizing opportunities to leverage your influence in support of others, and unintentionally making common allyship mistakes, you'll be ready to quit after a few months.

Increasing your emotional competence is an essential skill that you need to develop immediately. Without being emotionally competent, you'll get into senseless arguments with people who aren't as "fired up" as you about allyship. You will begin to resent taking on the sometimes burdensome responsibility of educating others on how to behave and think more equitably.

Without a high level of emotional competence, you will burn out and slowly settle into a place of complacency for this work.

Overcoming these setbacks is easy if you start to think about your emotional triggers now. Somehow, somewhere, we began to buy-in to the narrative that having conversations related to diversity, equity, and inclusion topics are "tough". I can just hear you now, "But it is Dr. Brandi... it is hard." NO IT IS NOT. The topics themselves don't make DEI conversations tough, it's the people who you're having the conversation with that make it tough. The people who don't listen, the people who are always ready to argue, the people who will never apologize, the people who are defensive, the people who are angry at the world--the people with a low EQ. It's those people who make the conversations tough, and we must separate the topics from the people to push to a place of authentic allyship.

As an ally, you have a unique responsibility to be the bigger person at all times. To demonstrate the highest level of integrity, maturity, and emotional competence when you're at work and within your community. Others may not operate at the same level of excellence that I'm telling you is required, but that's none of your business. Your job is to be polished, poised, and positive at all times. To be clear, self-restraint and putting on a brave face isn't exactly what I'm talking about here. In order to be successful as an authentic ally, you must begin addressing your emotional triggers.

Emotional triggers are the behaviors of others that trigger a negative emotional response within you. We all have emotional triggers, but some of us respond more negatively to them than others. Being an ally for racial equity will require you to quickly become aware of the things that will trigger you. The behaviors, the reactions, the personality types etc. As you become aware of the triggers that could derail your ability to actively listen to others, to be empathetic, to respond appropriately to those who disagree with you, your effectiveness as an ally will be short lived.

Without addressing your emotional triggers, you will be stuck on an endless roller coaster of fear, offense, discouragement, bitterness, discontent, and even hatred. You'll feel like you're stuck in a weird nightmare where your "helpfulness" is always being misconstrued, where your intentions are being misunderstood, where your actions are unappreciated. To overcome these feelings, The Authentic Ally must do the work to get their emotions in check.

Here are a list of behaviors that I've observed in low EQ allies:

- Refusing to engage with people who have different points of view
- Consistently telling people that they are wrong for their personal views
- Making people feel guilty for who they are
- Demonizing people for being from a certain background
- Cutting people off during conversations
- Getting angry to the point of yelling at others
- Cutting people out of their lives for not actively becoming an ally for racial equity
- Rejecting people who don't show the same outward passion for racial equity work as they do
- Ostracizing colleagues who are from a certain background

- Using emotions rather than facts to substantiate their points
- Unfriending/unfollowing friends and family who don't use their social media to promote racial equity initiatives
- Consistently dominating the floor during conversations about racial equity
- Asking condescending questions to people who disagree with them
- Trying to be "right" during conversations
- Actively bullying, defaming, or publicly shaming people

If you've exhibited some of these behaviors in the past, don't feel bad about it, simply make a decision to do better from here on out. A willingness to iterate and adjust is a core skill that authentic allies must hone throughout their journey. If you observe these behaviors in other well-meaning allies, I'd recommend giving them a copy of this book (shameless plug!), but also sparking a conversation with them about how alternative behaviors can better support their goals. Rarely do people enter into a conversation with the intention of being disrespectful or hurtful. Many times, people are simply caught up in their emotions. Rather than writing someone off or avoiding them like the plague, try to engage with them around how their behavior may have negatively impacted their ability to get their point across. Make your feedback a kind of appeal to them. An appeal that makes it clear that you want to help them succeed. Only then, can we as allies help others attract more support for this cause.

#3 Knowledge- Am I culturally competent enough?

As an authentic ally, you have to assess your knowledge gaps and make a learning plan to effectively build your cultural competence. Attending a handful of webinars, reading a few articles, buying the latest book, and watching a documentary or two won't cut it.

Being culturally competent is not about memorizing behavioral "do's and don'ts" for how to interact with a certain group. It's about seizing opportunities to truly tune-in to the experiences of others. It's about orienting yourself toward a learning (not teaching) posture. The first step to building your cultural competence is identifying what you need to learn.

Be strategic here. Some of you may be thinking, "I have EVERYTHING to learn". Yes, but where should you start? What are the most interesting or relevant topics that are related to the allyship goals you would like to achieve? Are you interested in learning about African ancient history? Or maybe you want to delve into a more nuanced understanding of how the civil rights movement impacted America. Or, you may want to focus on the current business landscape of venture capital funding as it relates to the disparities in how Black women start-ups are funded. The sky's the limit. Never feel the pressure to learn about what everyone else is learning about. Don't let the trends guide your study.

Once you're clear about *what* you want to learn, it's time to find resources that have the information you need. Your sources are VERY important. These days, you can't trust everything that you find online, in schools, or even at the library. The Authentic Ally must be discerning before consuming random content that just **sounds** legitimate.

Here are some questions that you should consider asking yourself before continuing your cultural competence learning journey.

1. Who is the author or institution behind this content?

Do your due diligence to identify who the source of the content is. Who are they? What is their history? How long have they been creating content or thought leadership around the topic? What authority do they have in the space? Is there information anecdotal or research based? Are you listening to someone's personal experience or professional expertise? Do they have credentials? What are their credentials? Are they a scholar or practitioner?

2. What are their values? What is their thesis?

The Authentic Ally is aware of the various lenses that inform how people's DEI content is positioned. Is the author or institution more liberal/conservative? Do they believe in equity for all or equity for those who are "marginalized"? Do they believe that certain people have absolute privileges while others do not? Do their arguments focus largely on past issues, present issues, or future issues? Are they negatively oriented or more optimistic in their tone?

3. **Who are they funded by?**

For every inauthentic ally out there, there's an equally inauthentic company, agency, or organization capitalizing on the racial equity movement for marketing or visibility purposes. Some companies want to let their customers know that they are supportive so that they don't lose sales, not because they truly care about racial equity. In the recent past, we've seen public fallouts at some of the biggest retailers and corporations whose employees outed them for being disingenuous about their supposed interest in racial equity issues. Be mindful of racial equity propaganda too. It's out there and it's real. Beware.

When building your cultural competence, be mindful of what you're consuming and be willing to seek out information that refutes what you're used to reading. Stay open to alternative perspectives and remember that your goal should be sharpening your ability to look at one piece of information from a variety of different viewpoints. Having a comprehensive understanding of a few racial equity topics is more important than having a segmented understanding of lots of topics. Stay focused and go deep, not wide.

#4 Influence- How can I authentically help?

Authentic allies don't take cues from others on how to be an ally. They don't succumb to social media pressures to post certain messages or hashtags because everyone else is doing it. No virtue signaling here. Simply put, they don't perform.

As you strive to become an authentic ally, you have to identify the ways that you can authentically help. If you have a large and engaged social media following, you may actually choose to use your platform to bring awareness to a cause, but if you'd prefer making a private donation to a charitable organization, that's okay too. If you decide to leverage your power as a leader within your company, that is acceptable too. There are hundreds of ways that you can show up as an ally. The key is finding what authentically works for you.

Remember, focus on **your** allyship journey, not anyone else's. Don't get offended if you don't see other people's allyship actions. The Authentic Ally knows better than to put their faith in other people's actions. There are a lot of people and corporations who look like they care about racial equity. There are thousands of people who claim to be allies for racial equity, but behind the scenes they are the most inequitable people you'd ever meet. I don't want you to have a false sense of security that those who *look* like they're doing the right thing are true authentic allies. The more allies out there working on their own authenticity, the more progress we will make for this movement in the long-term.

Final Thoughts

These prerequisites are essential to building the character of an authentic ally. Remember, don't perform. Your journey is your journey. After you've acknowledged (and adjusted) your motives, your emotional triggers, your knowledge gaps, and your spheres of influence, you will have built a strong foundation for the future of your allyship journey.

CHAPTER 5

THE DOMAINS OF

AUTHENTIC ALLYSHIP

Many well-meaning allies are so frustrated right now-- they genuinely want to help, but they don't know where to start. And the ones who have started, have made minimal progress. They've read books, watched documentaries, and attended webinars and are still not sure how to take purposeful action. This issue creates an unnecessary insecurity for allies that often leads to an eventual decline in their efforts. Some may use what little energy they have left to continue posting on social media and attending a webinar here and there, but overall, the thrill eventually is gone.

After hearing from hundreds of well-meaning allies about their confusion, I got together with my colleague Emilio Osoria from CuriosityLed.com to discuss the possibility of taking both the quantitative and qualitative allyship data that my firm, the Calling All Allies Project collected to develop a model that could support allies in choosing a purposeful path for their allyship. What emerged from our work were three distinct Domains of Allyship. Think of each domain as representing an allyship journey or track that represents your "allyship style". You will naturally be attracted to either one track or another, however, over time you may realize that your "allyship style" changes based on a variety of different factors personal to you. The goal in presenting the first iteration of our Domains of Allyship, is to use them as a springboard for your subsequent allyship action. Each domain can be plotted within two dimensions: self/other awareness and high/low behavioral change. Remember, no one domain is better than another.

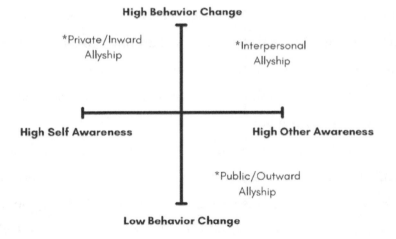

FIGURE 5.1
DOMAINS OF AUTHENTIC ALLYSHIP

High Behavior Change

*Private/Inward
Allyship

*Interpersonal
Allyship

High Self Awareness

High Other Awareness

*Public/Outward
Allyship

Low Behavior Change

Domain #1- Private/Inward Allyship

The private/inward allyship domain is characterized by someone who will need to have a high level of self- awareness and a high level of behavioral change. This ally is focused on two things: educating themselves and personal behavior change. Authentic allies who fall within this domain love to research new information about a variety of DEI topics. They feel more confident and comfortable with knowledge. Once they are equipped with information, they begin to adjust their behaviors accordingly. Understanding other worldviews and perspectives gives them the confidence they need to launch out into allyship long term.

It's important to note that allies who are most comfortable in this domain may not *look* like they're "doing" allyship. You may not even be able to tell right away that they're even an ally for racial equity, and that's okay. Remember, everyone's journey is personal to them. Don't fall into the trap that many inauthentic allies fall into, where they are working hard to educate themselves and change their behaviors, but they spend all of their time telling you about it; bragging about the latest book they've read and all of the handy dandy resources they've been bookmarking for future reference.

These allies are seeking attention. The authentic ally in the private/inward domain may never mention the work that they're doing behind the scenes..

59

Domain #2- Interpersonal Allyship

The interpersonal allyship domain is characterized by someone who wants to influence their immediate social circle. Unlike the private/inward allyship domain, the interpersonal allyship domain will require people who are high in other-awareness and who are willing to exhibit high behavioral change. These authentic allies have a knack for evangelizing. They get others excited about becoming allies for racial equity.

They take an empathic approach and seek first to understand others' perspectives so that they can share new knowledge, insights, and information about the racial equity movement and how people can get involved. These allies love group discussions about allyship and racial equity. Their allyship journey is enveloped in social interactions. They will share on social media, attend conferences, email resources to their network, and infuse insights from their allyship journey into as many conversations as they have. They will bring initiatives to their employers, join equity and inclusion committees and be a visible supporter for this cause.

Domain #3- Public/Outward Allyship

The Public/Outward Allyship domain is characterized by someone who is willing to use their personal resources or influence to directly support a person, cause, or effort. The public/outward domain is all about formal and informal influence. This ally will donate to a **reputable** organization or foundation that has a **proven track record** for positively impacting **legitimate** racial equity related causes. They will tap their network and support someone in need of business or career help. They will publicly endorse someone for a new role or position. They will write that letter of recommendation for a student; they will put their name and reputation on the line to help someone else advance. These authentic allies are less focused on learning and personal behavior change (private/inward domain), or galvanizing others around this cause (interpersonal domain). They seek opportunities to use their formal influence, power, money, or resources, to connect with the people who need it the most.

Final Thoughts

Remember, no one domain is more important than another. It's about you identifying the domain that best fits your style, interests, and personal passion for racial equity. The sooner you identify a starting point for your allyship journey the sooner you will be able to find opportunities to take purposeful action and sustain that action over time. Less doing more being.

Activate Your Allyship

Congratulations! You've made it this far and now it's time to create your personal plan to take purposeful action as an ally for racial equity. This plan is just a guide. You can adjust it at any time and can even adapt it to fit your journey as you become more confident and as your impact increases. Revisit this plan semi-annually to keep your allyship journey relevant and fresh.

First thing on your list? Select your allyship domain. Select your primary allyship domain then select 3-4 actions that you are committed to taking within the next 6 months.

Select one below.

⬜   Domain #1- Private/Inward Allyship

⬜   Domain #2- Interpersonal Allyship

⬜   Domain #3- Public/Outward Allyship

Allyship Domain Actions

Domain:	Start Date:
Month 1	Month 4
Month 2	Month 5
Month 3	Month 6

GET CLEAR ON YOUR MOTIVES

Instructions

Write a list of the reasons why you want to be an ally for racial equity. Let it sit for a day or two, then revisit the list. Review your motives and make sure that they aren't superficial or self-serving. Spend a week realigning yourself to more authentic motives that are true to who you are and what you believe. Create a final list and put them on a sticky note, or in a note in your phone so that you can reference them and hold yourself accountable if you begin to forget your "why?".

AUTHENTIC MOTIVES

Initial Brainstorm: List 5-7 reasons why you want to be an ally for racial equity.

Final List: Narrow your list down to only 2 reasons.

YOUR EMOTIONAL TRIGGERS

During your allyship journey you will be tested, disrespected, and triggered numerous times. To combat the discouragement that's common amongst well-meaning allies, you will need to take some time to address your emotional triggers. The things that can quickly derail your commitment to being an ally for racial equity.

Instructions

Answer the questions in the next section as honestly and thoroughly as possible. Think of this process as an emotional triggers audit. It will help you prepare for times when you will be tempted to get defensive and lash out or shut down when faced with challenging moments.

EMOTIONAL TRIGGERS

What behaviors of others could trigger a negative emotional response from you? (Identify 2)

What negative emotions do these behaviors trigger within you? (ex. anger, frustration, etc.)

Emotional Triggers cont'd

After experiencing the negative emotions identified above, how do you typically respond? (ex. shut down, lash out, etc.)

Emotional Triggers Cont'd

What emotionally competent response can you choose to exhibit?

What positive impact will your new response have on your allyship journey?

Emotional Triggers cont'd

How else can you cope with the stresses that may come from becoming an ally for racial equity?

YOUR CULTURAL COMPETENCE

Write a list of questions that you have about diverse groups. You can think beyond race and ethnicity as well. Remember, people are more than the color of their skin. Consider questions that you have about the disabled veteran's experience, or the adult with cognitive disabilities, for example. We each represent so many dimensions of diversity that it's important for authentic allies to look at the intersections of the various aspects of who people are.

CULTURAL COMPETENCE

What questions have you always wanted to know about the Black/African American or African culture?

Cultural Competence cont'd

What questions have you always wanted to know about Asian/Asian American cultures?

Cultural Competence cont'd

What questions have you always wanted to know about Latino/Central and South American cultures?

Cultural Competence cont'd

What questions have you always wanted to know about European/White American cultures?

Cultural Competence cont'd

List 5-7 reputable sources that produce information and content that can help you increase your cultural competence.

AUTHENTICALLY

Cultural Competence cont'd

FILL IN YOUR OWN-

FILL IN YOUR OWN-

Having "Authentic Allyship" Conversations

As you develop your allyship strategy and mature along your journey, you will need to master the art of having *authentic* allyship conversations. Authentic conversations create a constructive environment for you and others to develop your cultural competence. Authentic conversations build trust, mutual respect, and lead toward the goal of allyship—common ground. When two or more people reach common ground, they can navigate their differences with a level of maturity that opens the door for deeper understanding and deeper respect.

4 Steps of Authentic Allyship Conversations

Step 1- Identify the Purpose of the Conversation

The question I receive most frequently is, "how do you have conversations with people who are resistant to learning about racial equity?". My response is usually the follow-up question, "what is your purpose for having conversations with people who are 'resistant' to learning about racial equity?". To this question, I typically receive a response like, "To help them see that *they* are a part of the problem. If they don't see a problem, how can they be a part of the solution?"

This is yet another cognitive distortion that impedes well-meaning allies from being impactful in this movement. To overcome this limiting perspective, I recommend that you clearly identify your purpose for having a conversation with people about racial equity. Remember, people will change when they are ready to change and not a moment sooner. This is also true about you.

You and I are not responsible for forcing people to 'get it'. We are not responsible for accelerating the time it takes for people to change their minds about certain issues. When you initiate an interpersonal interaction with a goal of changing the other "wrong" person, you are already putting yourself at a disadvantage. You will not be successful. Rather, you will most likely leave angry, frustrated, and with a more damaged relationship than you had before the conversation began. You should enter conversations about racial equity with a purpose of gaining a better understanding and helping the other person gain a better understanding—not change. If you have any other motive, you will struggle to attract other allies to this movement, and you will do more harm than good.

Step 2- Respect the Relational Context

The success of authentic allyship conversations is increased when the two individuals have a mutually respectful relationship. Unfortunately, today's inauthentic allies continuously stumble from one failed conversation to the next because they don't understand the power of relationships. Imagine how counterproductive a conversation would be, if a person skips step one (identify the purpose), and couples that with a lack of regard for the relational context of the interaction. Simply put, you cannot attempt to engage in a conversation with a person who: 1) you have just met, or 2) you do not have a mutually respectful relationship with.

I advise countless professionals who are exhausted and defeated because of numerous failed interactions they've had with people who are so 'resistant' to change. When I ask who these 'resistant' people are, the inauthentic ally shares that they are people from social media, or family members whom they already have strained relationships with. Why on earth would they think that a conversation about racial equity would be successful if they don't even have good relationship with the people they are interacting with?

I recommend that you avoid having 1-on-1 conversations about racial equity with:

- People you genuinely don't like
- People you have a strained relationship with
- People who you don't know
- People who you do not have a close relationship with

- People who you perceive as "wrong" or "bad" for their views

Step 3- Listen with a Goal of Understanding the Other Person
Motivating people to adapt their mindset is an art, not a science, and it is definitely not a fight. If you approach conversations about racial equity with a win-lose orientation, you will **lose** every time. The goal should never be to prove your point or show the other person how wrong they are. The goal should be to increase your understanding of where the other person is coming from so that you can be strategic about how to educate them about your point of view. If you understand where they are coming from, you may find a point of common ground to help them understand your perspective.

This can be challenging for Authentic Allies in-the-making who are still emotionally triggered by various racial equity topics. Until you can heal from your own past hurts, traumas, and dysfunctions, you will not be able to engage in productive authentic allyship conversations. Be willing to leave the conversation without a clear indication that the other person has changed their perspective. It may take hours, days, or even months for something that you said to "click" for them. Your goal is to plant seeds that they can go and water during their personal allyship journey.

Step 4- Assess the Conversation, Take Purposeful Action, and Iterate Your Strategy

After the conversation is over, you should immediately reflect upon the interaction. Identify what went well and what did not. Write down any new knowledge that you learned. Create a list of additional cultural competence building resources that you may need to revisit. This brain dump will help you find perspective about the conversation in an accelerated way. Resist the urge to immediately call someone else to tell them how good or bad the conversation went. Simply reflect independently and give yourself time to debrief and develop your own understanding.

Your next step is to take purposeful action. What did you learn from the conversation? How will you change your approach in future conversations? What new information do you need to share with others in your network? What changes will you make to your daily lifestyle? Taking action is one of the most important aspects of being an authentic ally. Nowadays, there is too much talking and not enough doing. Conversations will not spark positive change for the racial equity movement—action will.

Final Thoughts on Authentic Allyship Conversations

Every Authentic Ally must prepare themselves for conversations about their journey, racial equity, and reaching common ground to support all communities. Authentic Allies must understand the power that they have to push this movement forward. Every failed conversation could hinder another prospective ally from joining the movement. One emotional outburst can close people off to helping this cause. Keep this in mind before you put your personal issues above the importance of this movement. Maturity and humility are skills that you must hone to support this movement for years to come. Get off your moral high horse and come down into the trenches of Authentic Allyship. Remember, if it were easy, everyone would be doing it.

YOUR ALLYSHIP HAS BEEN ACTIVATED!

Dear Authentic Ally,

Congrats on making it to the end of Authentic Ally! I hope that you expanded your idea of what it means to be an ally for racial equity. I hope that at least one concept planted a seed that you can now water through your purposeful action. I hope that you are motivated and more confident to own your allyship journey. If you can say, 'yes' to any of those things, I have done my job.

If you need any additional support, email me directly at contact@doctorbrandi.com or connect with me on LinkedIn at www.LinkedIn.com/in/thedoctorbrandi. This is only the beginning of your journey and my work around allyship. Let us continue the discussion and build upon this foundation together.

In excellence,

Dr. Brandi

ABOUT THE AUTHOR

BRANDI M. BALDWIN, PHD

Dr. Brandi M. Baldwin is a psychology and business professor turned entrepreneur who is a thought leader and author tackling the world's most relevant business challenges: diversity and inclusion, motivating millennials to level-up their leadership, and advocating for equity in all levels of business.

As the CEO of Millennial Ventures Holdings and a respected Wharton Lecturer, Dr. Brandi also hosts the "Diversity and Confusion" podcast and the "Leader-ish Podcast". She is the founding visionary for Calling All Allies Project (CAAP), a DEI innovation and organizational equity firm that empowers organizations to address their commitment to equity by making necessary, positive change in the areas where culture and climate intersect with Diversity, Equity & Inclusion (DEI).

Dr. Brandi is a published author and speaks at over 40 conferences and companies annually. She is tapped by companies such as Comcast, Discover, and the Federal Government to share her unconventional insights on leadership, diversity and inclusion, and business. Her noteworthy accomplishments include being appointed to Philadelphia Mayor Jim Kenney's Millennial Advisory Commission, being named one of Philadelphia's Most Influential

African Americans, receiving Philadelphia Business Journal's 40 Under 40 award, the Diversity and Inclusion Outstanding Ally honor from the Philadelphia Inquirer, and the "Take the Lead" award from the Girl Scouts. Dr. Brandi earned her doctorate in Educational Leadership & Policy Studies from Temple University and holds a master's degree in Adult & Organizational Development.

Dr. Brandi is the author of "Put in Work: Gain Respect, Influence Others, and Get Results as a New Leader", and "Authentic Ally: Ditch the Guilt, Stop Performing, and Take Purposeful Action as an Ally for Racial Equity". She is a mother of two and attributes her Christian faith for keeping her focused, grounded, and committed to excellence in all that she does. Although her worldly accomplishments are noteworthy, Dr. Brandi believes that she was put on this earth to impact, not to impress.

To learn more about her thought leadership, authorship, and speaking visit www.DoctorBrandi.com.

ACKNOWLEDGMENTS

Thank you to everyone who has supported my DEI work and the development of this book. To the entire team at the Calling All Allies Project, thank you for believing in my vision and working tirelessly to help our firm #IgniteWorkplaceUnity in the midst of there being so much negativity and opposition attached to this work.

Thank you, Emilio Osoria, for helping me to execute the vision for CAAP. Your wisdom, guidance, patience, and accountability have been a tangible part of our business success. Thank you for reminding me of your number one rule... "stay curious"!

I'd like to acknowledge some amazing allies who have helped me along this journey: Jerry C. Wells Jr. from Keller Williams, Jerilyn Dressler for consistently connecting me with opportunities, Erica Wexler, my strategic partner in impact, Tonya Ladipo, one of the best DEI consultants who specializes in African American wellness, Lilly Spantidaki an international ally who always looks for opportunities to support my work, to Nick, Victoria and Chris from the fun dept., you all are the best partners we've had, and to the entire DiverseForce team who have supported my work for years, thank you for all that you do. Thank you to Patty Jackson and Stephanie LeBlanc-Godfrey from Google for interviewing me for the book launch.

Thank you to the publishing team at Leader-ish Media Group, and to Krisburt Ballesteros for putting the finishing touches on this project.

Thank you to the companies around the world who have trusted my thought leadership and innovative approach to guide some of your toughest DEI projects. Our partnerships will never be forgotten. Kudos to taking the steps required to #IgniteWorkplaceUnity within your organizations.

I have to thank my family and friends. To them, I'm not "Dr. Brandi", I'm just "Bran." From my Jamaican and Guyanese father to my African American mother, my Puerto Rican cousins, and my friends from all over the world, thank you for keeping me grounded. Thank you for showing me grace. Thank you for allowing me to show up exactly the way that I am. Thank you for telling me what I NEED to hear, even if I may not want to hear it. Thank you for praying for me, encouraging me, and wiping my tears away. Thank you for not allowing me to get depressed or discouraged while navigating the front lines of DEI. Thank you for helping me to understand the greater reason why I do this work. Your strength and support are much appreciated.

Finally, I'd like to thank my children. Thank you for loving me unconditionally. Thank you for being a constant reminder of why I work so hard. I will do whatever it takes to ensure that the world that you live in is better off because I've been in it. Enjoy your life, walk with a spirit of love, pray for your enemies, and never forget that your life matters. Mommy loves you.

To learn more about the diversity, equity, and inclusion work of Dr. Baldwin and her team, visit www.CallingAllAllies.com.

Made in the USA
Middletown, DE
02 September 2024

60283727R00056